WHAT'S YOUR EXCUSE?

WHAT'S YOUR EXCUSE?

Over 100 Excuses from People Who Were
Stopped for Speeding

By

Dominick T. Andrews

Traffic Officer

RIVERCROSS PUBLISHING, INC.
New York • Orlando

Copyright © 1998 by Dominick T. Andrews

ISBN:1-58141-000-X

Library of Congress Catalog Card Number:98-13300

First Printing

Library of Congress Cataloging-in-Publication Data

Andrews, Dominick T., 1962-
    What's your excuse? : over 100 excuses from people who were stopped for speeding / by Dominick T. Andrews.
        p.   cm.
    ISBN 1-58141-000-X
    1. Excuses--Humor. 2. Speed limits--Humor. I. Title
PN6231.E87A53   1998
818'.5402--dc21   98-13300
                                                CIP

I dedicate this book to Tonyia, Dominick and Sydney.

Preface

After my first six months working as a traffic officer on a police department in the south, I must have listened to more than 100 excuses that drivers offered when they were stopped for speeding. With over 2400 citations written a year, I have heard some excuses that were truly original, most that were laughable, and some that warranted my compassion. As for the rest of them, I would just say to myself, "Tell it to the judge."

Most of the drivers I encountered gave me no excuse and humbly accepted their traffic citation. Others became irritable, arrogant, belligerent, abrupt, argumentative, or cried their eyes out. And if you thought that a man wouldn't cry when given a ticket–well, some do!

Along with the excuses, there were a few female drivers who had the crazy idea that if they exposed certain body parts I wouldn't give them a ticket. Well, thanks for the side show, but it doesn't work on me. I even had one driver who was so distraught about getting a ticket that she stuck her head out the window of her car and vomited on my shoes. And believe it or not, some drivers actually said, "Thank you," and shook my hand.

I hope you enjoy these excuses as much as I did. But please don't try to use them on the officer who might stop you for speeding. He has probably heard them before!

WHAT'S YOUR EXCUSE?

What's Your Excuse?

1. I was trying to pull my sun visor down. 73mph/55mph

2. I was on my way to wash my car. 67mph/30mph

3. If you'll forget about it, I won't do it again. 50mph/30mph

4. I'm a pastor and I'm late to coach a basketball game. 55mph/35mph

5. I'm on my way to dispose of my father's ashes. 73mph/55mph

6. Huh! 83mph/55mph

7. What are you operating, a speed trap? 50mph/30mph

8. I'm on my way to see my mom in the hospital. 67mph/35mph

9. My daughter spilled chocolate ice cream on herself. 64mph/45mph

10. I'm late for work at DOMINOS. 89mph/55mph

11. I've never driven in this state before.
    64mph/45mph

12. I have a patient lying open on the table at
    the hospital. 58mph/35mph

13. It's a new transmission. 66mph/45mph

14. I thought the speed limit was 65.
    79mph/55mph

15. My tooth hurts. 42mph/25mph

16. It's the tires. 76mph/50mph

17. I had to pass the bus. 54mph/30mph

18. Officer, I'm on my way to meet with a
    study group to study for the Bar and if I
    get a ticket, I'll have to resubmit my Bar
    application. Please show me some mercy
    and don't give me a ticket.
    53mph/35mph.

19. I had a CD player installed by Circuit City
    and they must have shorted out my
    speedometer because every time I hit a
    bump, it doesn't work. 57mph/35mph

20. I was simply following all the traffic ahead
    of me. 63mph/35mph

"You Should Be Out Catching Burglars Or Something"

One fall evening, I clocked a vehicle going at a speed of 67mph in a posted 30mph zone from a distance of half a mile. I figured that if he didn't see me, he would at least be in the mid 70's by the time he got to me. As the vehicle got closer, its speed was reduced dramatically. I guess he saw me sitting under the street lamp. After I stopped the vehicle and asked for license and proof of insurance, the driver started his lecture. I had no other choice but to stand there and let him berate me with all his might and immaturity. He told me that I was just picking on him and he wanted to know where I was on the night that his apartment was burglarized. He continued on and on as sarcastically as he could. He thought that my being out there stopping people for speeding was not as important as other things that I should be doing as a police officer and that I "Should be out catching burglars or something." I gave him his ticket and went on my way. I knew that I would get him again. I prayed that I would get him again.

Six months later, I was in the same spot and a vehicle was heading towards me traveling in the mid 50's. I pulled the vehicle over and guess what? It was my sarcastic friend again and I can't tell you how big the grin was on my face. He begged me not to give him the ticket. Of course, no excuse in the world would have changed my mind and I had to remind him of the tongue-lashing he had given me months previously. He didn't know what to say to me. As a matter of fact, he was quite humble. I went to my car, wrote the ticket and returned to his vehicle to issue him the summons. He was the first grown man I've ever seen cry when given a ticket.

The Bribe

One evening I had the occasion to stop a Ford Bronco for speeding through a residential neighborhood. The posted speed limit was 25 mph and the vehicle was clocked on radar at 46 mph. There were 5 people in the truck and the driver indicated that they had just left a party. I asked the driver for his license and insurance card and told him why I stopped him. I took his documents back to my patrol car and began to write out the ticket. While writing the ticket, I looked at the insurance card in its holder and noticed that behind the insurance card was what looked like the outer portion of paper money. I removed the insurance card and found a fifty dollar bill staring at me.

I put my ticket book down and returned to the driver. I said, "Sir, I think we might have a problem here." He asked me what it was and I asked him to explain to me why the fifty dollar bill was conveniently tucked behind the insurance card.

Well, let me tell you how quiet it got in that vehicle and you should have seen the expression on the driver's face. He immediately told me in a scared, stumbling voice that he kept the bill there for emergencies and just plain forgot about it when he handed me the insurance card holder.

His wife then interjected with, "That's the truth Officer, really!" There was a pause and then I looked at the driver and smiled.

I handed back the fifty, and told him he'd just had an emergency and that he'd probably need the fifty to pay the fine for his speeding ticket!

What's Your Excuse?

21. I was on my way to pick up my daughter from the baby-sitter's because I don't know if I can trust her with my daughter. 75mph/55mph

22. I was on my way to get a barbecue sandwich. 64mph/45mph

23. I just moved here and I've never driven on this road before. 49mph/25mph (school zone)

24. I didn't know if my brakes were working so I was checking them. 53mph/35mph

25. I just broke up with my boyfriend and I thought I was calm enough to drive. 53mph/35mph

26. I was taking Deputy Reilly's kids to day care. 63mph/25mph (school zone)

27. I have to go to the bathroom. 82mph/55mph

28. It wasn't me, I know it wasn't. It was the car ahead of me. 51 mph/35mph

29. We're late for school. 71mph/35mph

30   I'm drinking this barium and I have to get
      to the hospital in half an hour.
      50mph/35mph

31.   I'm delivering dinner and I don't want it to
      get cold. 50mph/35mph

32.   I'm trying to get to the health club before
      they close. 55mph/30mph

33.   I was on the way to the Post Office to drop
      the mail off. 52mph/30mph

34.   No reason. 58mph/35mph

35.   I was running late for work. 81
      mph/55mph

36.   I was talking to my wife. 51 mph/35mph

37.   I'm a Presbyterian Pastor and I'm late to
      teach a class. 50mph/35mph

38.   I was trying to get my cat home.
      48mph/35mph

39.   The pipes at my trailer are frozen and my
      husband told me to get to his work quick.
      54mph/35mph

40.   I thought the speed limit was 45.
      55mph/35mph

Out the Window

I was on the interstate and noticed a Mustang GT that was whipping along in the outside lane. I stopped the car after about a half mile and approached the driver. The driver had a radar detector and told me that there was no way that I could have caught him on radar because his radar detector didn't go off. I told him that I would go back to my car and activate my radar and that he should watch his detector. I activated the radar and I could see the LED display turn on from my vehicle. I went back to the driver, who was still dumbfounded as to why his detector didn't go off. I explained to him that I kept my antenna in a standby mode to defeat detectors. He put his hands to his face in disgust.

I went back to my car and started writing the ticket and, while looking up at one point I saw this arm swing out of the window and with it went the radar detector. It really made me laugh inside and I got out of my vehicle and walked over to the radar detector lying on the grass. I picked it up and handed it back to the driver. I told him that I was only writing him a warning about his speed, but that if he threw his radar detector out again I'd cite him for littering! He thanked me for the warning and said that he had learned his lesson.

What's Your Excuse?

41. I'm on the way to the office to try and be the tenth caller to win "Vince Gill" tickets. 52mph/30mph

42. I'm late to pick up my girlfriend. You know how women are when you're late. 54mph/35mph

43. I have to give this guy an estimate to paint his house and I was suppose to be there a while ago. 51 mph/35mph.

44. I'm late for swim practice. 60mph/35mph

45. I'm a locksmith and I'm late to help this lady open her car. 51 mph/35mph

46. I'm taking my two invalid aunts to the hairdresser. 67mph/45mph

47. I just got the car out of the shop and I'm checking it out to see if I can still hear the rattle. 44mph/25mph (school zone)

48. My dad just had bypass surgery and I'm on my way to get some groceries for my mom. 64mph/45mph

49. I was having a conversation with him and I wasn't paying attention. 66mph/45mph

Southern Exposure

It was a quiet Saturday morning and I was operating stationary radar on a main highway that entered our city limits. I was sitting on my motorcycle watching the sun rise when the pitch of my radar rose. I looked up at the road and started tracking the mid-sized vehicle coming towards me. The posted speed on this road was 50 mph and the vehicle passed me at 72 miles per hour. I pursued it.

After stopping the vehicle, I approached the driver and thought that this was the same person I stopped for running 63mph in a 35 mph zone about two weeks earlier. I asked her if I had stopped her before and she confirmed my suspicion.

I remember her telling me the first time that if I didn't give her a ticket, she wouldn't speed anymore. After taking her license and insurance card, I went back to my motorcycle and started writing the ticket. When I was done, I approached her, and when I looked into the car at her, I saw that she had unbuttoned her blouse and exposed her breasts to me. Obviously, I couldn't help but look–and smile in admiration. After all, this had never happened to me before. She smiled at me, and while I probably turned a nice shade of red, I didn't compromise my integrity and went ahead and handed her the summons. Her smile quickly turned into a frown as I gave her her second speeding ticket.

She buttoned up her blouse and said, "I guess you and I are never going to get along!"

Oh, well. But I never again had a reason to look at her car–or her breasts!

What's Your Excuse?

50. Officer, I really have to pee and if I don't get to the Conoco Station I'm going to burst. 55mph/35mph

51. The Sheriff Deputies were having a road check and traffic was backed up because of it and it caused me to be late. 68mph/45mph

52. You know how these old trucks are–can't trust the gauges. 57mph/35mph

53. I'm running these specimens back to the hospital because the doctor has labeled them wrong. 53mph/30mph

54. Just trying to get home from school. 66mph/35mph

55. Sorry! 61 mph/35mph

56. The cars ahead of me were traveling too slow. 53mph/35mph

57. I really didn't realize I was going that fast. 67mph/45mph

58. I was trying to get to the bank before they closed. 64mph/45mph

59. I'm late for work. 74mph/55mph

60. No reason, just trying to get to work. 80mph/55mph

61. Trying to get to my softball game. 50mph/15mph

62. I'm trying to get my grandbaby to day care. 52mph/25mph

63. I want to see the radar! Never mind, JUST GIVE ME THE TICKET!! 54mph/25mph

64. I was trying to catch up to somebody. 48mph/25mph

65. I'm the assistant principal at PS 441 and I just gave blood and I'm late getting back to school. 47mph/25mph

66. I've got a migraine headache and I was trying to pass around two cars that were stopped in the road. 51 mph/25mph

67. You got me! 67mph/45mph

68. I didn't know that was the speed limit. 64mph/35mph

69. I just left a heart patient at the hospital and I'm trying to get back to my office because they keep paging me and I'm late. 56mph/35mph

I've Been a Lawyer for 40 Years

I stopped an attorney for speeding one day, and when I initially engaged in a conversation with him he was quite polite and told me all about how he was an attorney and had been practicing law for over 40 years. He also made it a point to tell me that he had never gotten a ticket before because he knew most of the officers on the police department. Well, he didn't know me and quite frankly, his comments offended me. I wrote out the ticket and as I was writing it, he told me in a very agitated, degrading manner that I was an embarrassment to the department and that I didn't know who I was messing with. I stood there and took his insults and, after handing him the ticket, I went and set back up for the next car.

The very next day I was set up in the same spot and initiated a traffic stop on a vehicle for running 44mph in the 25mph zone. Well, this driver happened to be the wife of the attorney who reamed me out the day before. I gave her the ticket and thought to myself, wait until this lady gets home and tells her husband that I gave her a ticket too. It still wasn't over.

A week later, I was on the same road and I got the attorney's wife a second time. This time, she was as rude as he was the first time and of course, I did not hesitate to ticket her again.

I wondered if this "legal eagle" and his wife would go to court to try to fight the fines. Well they did. He represented his wife and both maintained their innocence. The judge found both of them guilty!

What's Your Excuse?

70. My foot got stuck between the accelerator and the clutch. 48mph/25mph

71. Are you sure that the lights were on? 45mph/25mph (School Zone)

72. Giving me a ticket doesn't mean that I'm going to stop speeding. 43mph/25mph

73. I'm late for an appointment at the mall. 60mph/30mph

74. I'm late for church. 51 mph/30mph

75. My mom's expecting me. 60mph/35mph

76. What did you stop me for? (May I see your driver's license and proof of insurance?) Why are you stopping me? (For speeding.) But I didn't even reach the posted speed on the Interstate! (But you did exceed the posted speed limit on Park Avenue. Now, may I see your drivers license and proof of insurance?) 52mph/30mph

77. I was trying to get my dog home. 52mph/30mph

78. I was trying to pass around the other car. 58mph/30mph

79. Not you again? 54mph/30mph

80. I'm sorry, I'm sorry. 59mph/35mph

81. I'm new down here. Anyway, I had to pass that car because he was moving into my lane. 55mph/35mph

82. My captain told me that I had to work another station and for me to get there as fast as I can. 60mph/35mph

83. I'm going between my two jobs. 63mph/35mph

84. I'm trying to get to Walmart so I can get some stuff to fix my tire. 67mph/30mph

85. I feel sick, I'm going to throw up, and I've got a migraine. 52mph/35mph

86. I'm taking the kids to baseball practice and I have to get to the doctor's office. 55mph/35mph

87. I'm on my way to take a final exam. 50mph/30mph

88. I just left the hospital. 51 mph/30mph

89. I just came off the interstate and accidentally hit resume on my cruise control. 55mph/35mph

Is That Your Bathing Suit?

Late one afternoon, I was operating radar in a residential neighborhood and stopped this Mazda for speeding. The driver was a female and when I came up to the side of her car, I noticed that she was scantly dressed. It appeared as if she was wearing a bra and panties. I thought to myself that it can't be and that it was just some type of bathing suit. I asked her for her license and insurance card. She gave me the license but was still searching for the insurance card. I went back to my patrol car with her license and began to write the ticket.

While writing the ticket, I looked up to write her license plate number on the citation. Just then, the driver stepped out of her car with what appeared to be her insurance card in hand. Well, guess what? That was no bathing suit she was wearing and you could see right through her bra and panties!

Within a matter of seconds, passing motorists were slowing their cars and trucks to get a glimpse of this young woman standing in the road with nothing on but her almost invisible underwear. I quickly got out of my car and expedited the traffic stop to get her back in her car. My face was as red as a cherry. Anyway, I really wanted to know her reason for not being dressed and so I asked her.

She told me. "Officer," she said, "I'm on my way to a party and the dress I'm going to wear is at my girlfriend's house. I didn't want to get dressed at home and then have to get undressed only to get dressed again."

What's Your Excuse?

90. I was trying to find a place to turn around. 54mph/35mph

91. I'm late for my rotation at the hospital. 54mph/30mph

92. I'm late for school. 60mph/35mph

93. I'm bringing some stuff to my mom in the hospital. 52mph/30mph

94. I was trying to pass around those cars so I could get over. 56mph/30mph

95. My car won't go up hill if I don't speed up. 50mph/30mph

96. We're on our way to the mall to pick out wedding dresses. 47mph/25mph

97. I'm on my way home from a funeral and my speedometer isn't working. 45mph/25mph

98. I wasn't paying attention. 57mph/25mph

99. I forgot to put on deodorant and was on my way to get some at the drug store before I go to work. 55mph/35mph

100. I was trying to get home to my 6-day-old baby. 53mph/25mph

101. I'm trying to get home to empty this bag on my chest. 60mph/30mph

102. I'm trying to get to the library. 52mph/30mph

103. I'm a private investigator and I got called to go find this guy at the school. 53mph/25mph

104. I'm meeting my classmates for a study group at Burger King. 64mph/45mph

105. I'm late for class at the law school. 56mph/30mph

106. Officer, I've got real bad cramps and I'm trying to get home to take some medicine. 51mph/35mph

107. The light that illuminates my speedometer wasn't working. 50mph/30mph

108. I was only doing 65 when I saw you. This is April Fool's, right? 75mph/55mph

109. I was just testing out my new Mitsubishi Turbo. You know it can go 150mph? 63mph/35mph

110. I must have had my head up my butt. 56mph/40mph

The Miscarriage of Justice

I was on the interstate late one morning and tracked a Jeep Cherokee traveling in the fast lane. I estimated it to be running in the 90's. Just after the driver became aware of me you could see the nose of the vehicle dip down harshly towards the pavement as a result of the brakes being depressed hard. Even after seeing the vehicle dip down, I still recorded it on the radar at 87 mph.

I pulled the vehicle over and the excuse the driver gave me was that she was bleeding and was having a miscarriage. She said she was on her way to the hospital. I really didn't believe her so I told her that I would follow her to the emergency room. She said that she didn't need me to do that , but I insisted. I think she knew I was on to her.

But before I got back into my car she told me that she first had to go to her apartment to get her insurance card. So now I'm thinking, if this is such an emergency, I would go straight to the hospital. Well, I followed her to her apartment and I guess she thought that I wouldn't stay with her all this time. You could tell by her demeanor that she wasn't having a miscarriage. So, she said to me that she was going to the hospital and that I didn't have to follow her there. Of course, I insisted on the escort.

Anyway, I followed her to the hospital and was able to get into the emergency room before she did. I spoke with the nurse there and told her to expect this girl with the miscarriage and that I thought she was bluffing it because I caught her speeding, The driver came in and was escorted into one of the treatment rooms. Several minutes later the nurse came out and smiled. She said that the driver wasn't even pregnant and had confided to the nurse that she had lied in order to avoid the ticket. The nurse said that it would have been less expensive for her to pay the ticket then to have admitted herself to the emergency room.

Of course I had to present her with the speeding ticket anyhow.

What's Your Excuse?

111. I was looking down at my pager.
54mph/35mph

112. I have no idea how fast I was going because I was talking to my husband on this damn car phone. 59mph/40mph

113. I was trying to get a CD from between my legs. 81mph/55mph

114. I was trying to get the car back home so my father could go to work.
57mph/25mph

115. I'm a florist and I have to purchase these flowers before 11 o'clock. 47mph/25mph

116. This is my first time home in a couple of months. 65mph/35mph

117. I wasn't going that fast. 59mph/35mph

118. I guess I wasn't paying attention.
79mph/45mph

119. I'm on my way to Bible class.
53mph/35mph

120. What? Was I speeding? 54mph/30mph

121. I just had this upper G.I. and I'm on my way to my sister's because I'm sick. 66mph/45mph

122. I have distemper. 74mph/45mph

123. I guess I forgot to take my foot off the accelerator. 66mph/45mph

123. I was trying to dry my car off because I just washed it. 66mph/45mph

124. I just got done servicing my computer at Sears. 65mph/24mph

125. I was trying to cool myself off because there's no air conditioning in this car. 79mph/55 mph

126. I can't believe you got me. I thought I knew all the spots you guys hide out. 67mph/45 mph

127. It just felt like one of those days I could get away with it. 88mph/55 mph

128. I thought the speed limit was 70 so how about you knocking it down to just 14 over the speed limit and we'll call it even. 80mph/55 mph

129. I was just trying to get home to watch the Andy Griffin marathon. 68mph/45mph

Spit-Shined Shoes

I have never in my life seen a woman so distressed over a speeding ticket as this one lady. I stopped this lady late one evening for speeding. After speaking with her, I determined that she was in violation of several other traffic laws. I told her that I would issue warnings for those but a ticket for the speeding.

I returned to my car, wrote the ticket and went to issue her the summons. By this time, she was crying so hard that she couldn't talk to me without choking on her tears. I tried to calm her down. I explained to her that it could have been a lot worse and that she was only getting just the one ticket. I asked her to please stop crying because she was really working herself up and I was concerned for her.

I gave her the ticket and the warnings and went back to my car and waited for her to drive off. I sat there for about five minutes and she still didn't drive away. I got out of my car and approached her. She was still crying hard and it almost seemed as if she were hyperventilating. I told her that I wished she would calm down and that I was going to have to stay with her until she got back on the road.

You should have seen this poor lady. She was trying so hard to tell me that she was going to be all right but she couldn't because of how hard she was crying and gasping. I said, "Ma'am, please move on." And as I stood there, she stuck her head out the car window and vomited all over my shoes. After that, she put the car in gear and drove off!

What's Your Excuse?

130. I just had my car painted and I was trying to beat the storm. 63mph/35mph

131. Lousy radar detector. 78mph/55mph

132. That old lady ahead of me was going so slow that I had to pass around her because she was driving me nuts. 54mph/35mph

133. But the speed limit sign said 75. (No, that was the sign for Interstate 75.) 82mph/55mph

134. I was riding my brakes. 59mph/40 mph

135. These aren't my stomping grounds. 56mph/35 mph

136. The lady ahead of me was putting her makeup on. 55mph/35 mph

137. I forgot my license at the shop and I was going back to get it. 83mph/55 mph

138. I just ran over a dead skunk and I was trying to get away from the smell. 67mph/35 mph

139. I can't have been going 76. My mechanic said this car couldn't go that fast. 76mph/55 mph

140. My wife found out that I was at a strip club and if I'm not home in 10 minutes, she is going to shoot my truck. 82mph/55 mph

141. I've got real bad diarrhea and cramps. 48mph/25 mph

142. I accidentally stuck my eye with my eye-liner brush. 57mph/35 mph

143. The IRS waits for no one. 62mph/30 mph

144. I couldn't downshift because I just had my nails done. See! 65mph/40 mph

145. I just left the vet and as you can see my dog threw up all over my seat. 69mph/50 mph

146. I had to pass that chicken truck. I couldn't stand the smell anymore. 60mph/35mph

147. I guess my mind was still on that Hooter's billboard. 78mph/55 mph

148. I was just cruising and listening to the radio. 48mph/25mph

149. I just came off that hill. 64mph/25 mph

A Family Affair

I was operating radar in a posted 30mph zone when I clocked a vehicle coming towards me at 51 mph. I stopped the car and spoke to the driver who stated that she was late for some church function. She was really pleasant, apologized and after being issued the ticket, and went on her way. I went around the corner and set up again for the next vehicle. All in all it took me about five minutes.

The very next vehicle speeding towards me was a vehicle identical to the one I had just stopped. I thought to myself, "Can this be that same lady speeding again?" The car was the same and the license plate looked the same, so I initiated a traffic stop. When I walked abreast of the driver's door, I saw a man in the driver's seat. I thought to myself, "Well, I guess she wouldn't have been that dumb to come down the same road at the same speed again. I asked the driver for his license and his last name was that of the lady I had just stopped previously. I asked him if he knew the lady and he said, "Why yes, that's my wife."

I said, "I'm sorry to say this but I just gave her a ticket for speeding a few minutes ago and I thought that you were she again."

He mused, "I guess when I get to the church, which is where she went, I'm going to see how long it is before she tells me she got a ticket."

I issued the driver the ticket and as I walked away, a thought occurred to me. I stopped and returned to the vehicle. I asked the driver, "By the way, you don't have any more family members coming down this same way, do you?" We both laughed, and he drove away–slowly.